20th Century
PERSPECTIVES

# Weapons and Technology of
# World War I

Paul Dowswell

Heinemann
LIBRARY

**H** www.heinemann.co.uk/library
Visit our website to find out more information about Heinemann Library books.

To order:
☎ Phone 44 (0) 1865 888066
📄 Send a fax to 44 (0) 1865 314091
💻 Visit the Heinemann Bookshop at www.heinemann.co.uk/library to browse our catalogue and order online.

First published in Great Britain by Heinemann Library,
Halley Court, Jordan Hill, Oxford OX2 8EJ,
a division of Reed Educational and Professional Publishing Ltd.
Heinemann is a registered trademark of Reed Educational and Professional Publishing Ltd.

OXFORD MELBOURNE AUCKLAND
JOHANNESBURG BLANTYRE GABORONE
IBADAN PORTSMOUTH (NH) USA CHICAGO

Produced for Heinemann Library by Discovery Books Limited
Designed by Sabine Beaupré
Illustrations by Mark Franklin
Maps by Stefan Chabluk
Consultant: Stewart Ross
Originated by Dot Gradations
Printed by Wing King Tong in Hong Kong

ISBN 0 431 11995 3
05 04 03 02
10 9 8 7 6 5 4 3 2 1

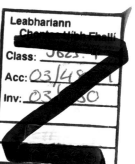

**British Library Cataloguing in Publication Data**
Dowswell, Paul 1957–
  Weapons and technology of World War I. – (20th century perspectives)
  1. World War, 1914–1918 – Equipment and supplies – Juvenile literature
  I. Title
  623.4'09041

**Acknowledgements**
The publishers would like to thank the following for permission to reproduce photographs:
Corbis, pp. 5, 7, 8, 9, 10, 11, 12, 13, 14, 16, 17, 18, 20, 22, 23, 24, 27, 29, 31, 32, 34, 36 (bottom), 37, 38, 40, 41, 42, 43; Hulton Getty, pp. 4, 15, 19, 21, 26, 39; Peter Newark's Pictures, 25, 28, 33, 35, 36 (top).

Cover photograph reproduced with permission of Corbis.

Every effort has been made to contact copyright holders of any material reproduced in this book. Any omissions will be rectified in subsequent printings if notice is given to the publishers.

Any words appearing in the text in bold, **like this**, are explained in the glossary.

# Contents

A century of war                                    4

World War One begins                                6

Trench warfare                                      8

Life in the trenches                               10

Uniforms, rifles and bayonets                      12

Other weapons of trench warfare                    14

Machine guns                                       16

The power of artillery                             18

Using the new artillery                            20

Poisonous gas                                      22

Transport                                          24

Tanks                                              26

Mighty warships                                    28

Submarines                                         30

Aeroplanes                                         32

Airships                                           34

Communications                                     36

Medicine                                           38

The cost of the war                                40

The war to end all wars                            42

Timeline                                           44

Further reading and places of interest             45

Glossary                                           46

Index                                              48

# A century of war

World War One began in 1914 and ended in 1918. Today, hardly any of the soldiers and **civilians** caught up in the conflict are still living. Yet the battles they fought and the horrors they endured still haunt us. On the Western and Eastern fronts (the areas of conflict between opposing armies) and at other major battlegrounds, men were killed in hitherto unheard of numbers.

## Changing technology

One reason for the terrible number of deaths was a change in weapons and other military **technology** over the previous hundred years. This change completely altered the face of warfare.

An earlier era of warfare had ended at the Battle of Waterloo, Belgium, in 1815. Under the eyes of commanders who could survey the whole field of battle, 72,000 French soldiers fought a combined army of over 100,000 British, Prussian and other troops. The armies faced each other in tightly drilled squares, their uniforms brightly coloured. Their **bayonets** were attached to single-shot guns called **muskets**. Their **artillery** fired muzzle-loaded, or front-loaded, cannon balls. **Cavalry** soldiers were the ultimate weapon, waiting a distance from the fighting and ready to charge in the hope that the enemy **front line** would scatter or crumble before them.

*The Battle of Waterloo, seen here, heralded the end of an earlier era of warfare. Throughout the rest of the 19th century, every large conflict brought developments in weapons and technology.*

## New directions

About 35 years later, there followed a series of armed conflicts that pointed warfare in a new direction. In the Crimean War (1853–56) **rifles** were used instead of muskets. Their grooved **barrels** gave both greater accuracy and range. In the American Civil War (1861–65) barbed wire was first used at the front. The Franco-Prussian War (1870–71) introduced the first machine guns. The Boer War (1899–1902) saw widespread use of rifles fitted with a **magazine** which contained several shots, so the gun did not need to be reloaded each time it was fired. New artillery was also developed, with a much higher rate of fire and accuracy. Finally, the Russo-Japanese War (1904–05) saw the first use of field telephones on the battlefront, huge **howitzer** guns and giant armoured battleships.

All these technological advances meant weapons were deadlier than they had ever been before. And the armies of certain countries had grown much larger and better organized. Opposing **empires** had become rivals in a struggle for power in Europe and beyond (see page 6). Many European nations of the early 20th century were increasingly hostile and suspicious of each other. They were also confident that if war did come, their new weapons would win them victory.

*In World War One, cavalry soldiers soon fell victim to enemy machine guns and artillery. This World War One cavalry unit was made up of men from India, then part of the British Empire.*

## Send in the cavalry

For thousands of years cavalry had been as important to armies as ordinary foot soldiers, or **infantry**. This was because the armed horsemen were fast and **manoeuvrable**. But in the face of the ferocious defensive weapons of World War One, cavalry charges were disastrous. There were some cavalry charges in western Europe at the start of the war. In one German charge against British troops, only 12 out the 70 horsemen survived.

Cavalry still had a part to play in other areas of the war, however, such as on the more open Eastern Front, and in the Middle East. In Palestine, for example, the Australian Light Horse and New Zealand Mounted Rifles were used very effectively against their Turkish enemies.

# World War One begins

This map shows how the nations and empires of Europe, North Africa and the Middle East allied themselves during World War One. Several battlefronts developed during the course of the conflict: the Western Front, the Eastern Front, the Balkan Front and the Middle Eastern Front.

## Rivalry between nations

When World War One began in 1914, Europe was already a continent divided by bitter rivalries over territory and military power. There were two main camps, each committed to defending other friendly nations. On one side were Germany, Austria-Hungary and the Ottoman **Empire** in an alliance known as the Central Powers. On the other were France, Russia and Britain in an alliance known as the Allies.

In June 1914, Archduke Franz Ferdinand of Austria-Hungary and his wife were killed by a Serbian assassin in Bosnia. (This was an area ruled by Austria-Hungary, but which Serbia wished to control.) Austria-Hungary declared war on Serbia, and Russia joined the war in Serbia's defence. The conflict then spread to most of the rest of Europe, as the other members of the rival power blocks were pulled into the war.

When the war began, Japan joined the Allies and attacked German **colonies** in the Far East. In 1915 Italy joined the Allies, and Bulgaria joined the Central Powers. Fighting also spread to German colonies in Africa, New Guinea and Samoa. The USA, in response to German

attacks on American ships, joined the Allies in 1917. By then, the war was being fought by nations from all over the world, although most of the fighting took place in Europe (on land and at sea) and in the Middle East.

## Trench tactics

Much of the warfare, at least on the Western Front, took place in trenches (protective ditches) from which armies launched attacks on each other. Trenches had first been used in this way in the American Civil War. The military planners of World War One based their approach to trench warfare on earlier conflicts, such as the Battle of Mukden in the Russo-Japanese War. The **casualties** of this four-week battle had been immense: 70,000 Japanese dead and 100,000 Russian dead. But despite their losses, the Japanese had eventually overwhelmed the Russian trenches. It seemed that all-out attack, whatever the casualties, would eventually win the day.

The World War One generals in Europe envisaged attacks by 'waves' of men moving close together in support of each other. Military thinking ruled out taking cover as troops neared enemy positions. It was thought that a steady advance in the face of heavy enemy fire actually produced fewer casualties. (Only towards the end of the war did such **tactics** change, when German stormtroopers – soldiers specially trained to attack – fought in smaller units, taking cover where necessary.)

*Allied troops on the Western Front in 1918, led by their commander, leave a trench as German **shells** burst around them. The military tactic of advancing steadily into the face of heavy fire cost countless lives.*

## Terrible lessons

In the early weeks of World War One, such thinking produced huge casualties. It quickly became clear that the weapons of defence, especially the machine gun which could fire a murderous 600 rounds a minute, were too good for such simple tactics.

As the **front lines** solidified into well-defended trenches, senior commanders on all sides found they were fighting a type of war of which they had no experience and no clear idea of how to win. In warfare, their training and experience told them, victory lay with the army that could seize ground from the enemy. If no one could seize ground from anyone else, how could the war be won? The generals spent the next four years trying to solve this problem. Tragically, some of their **strategies** and tactics were more suitable to the previous century, and resulted in dreadful slaughter.

# Trench warfare

### The Western Front

As attack and **counter-attack** ground to a halt in the autumn of 1914, French and British troops raced to the North Sea and Swiss border in an attempt to **outflank** the Germans, who were doing the same in the hope of outflanking the Allies. Both sides failed, and the result was the Western Front. The battlefront stretched 750 kilometres (466 miles) through Belgium and France's eastern border with Germany.

The Western Front soon developed into a complex series of opposing trenches. These **fortified** ditches had firing steps, sandbag protection, **parapets**, **dug-outs**, their own crude sanitary systems and even rail supply networks. Sometimes the gap between opposing trenches, known as 'no man's land', was a kilometre or more wide; sometimes it was as little as 50 metres. These types of fortifications were also used at Gallipoli and other fronts.

Between late 1914 and the spring of 1918, millions of lives were lost on the Western Front trying to break through enemy trenches. But in all that time the front line never moved more than 16 kilometres (10 miles) one way or the other. The trenches, with their machine gun and barbed wire defences, had become virtually impregnable.

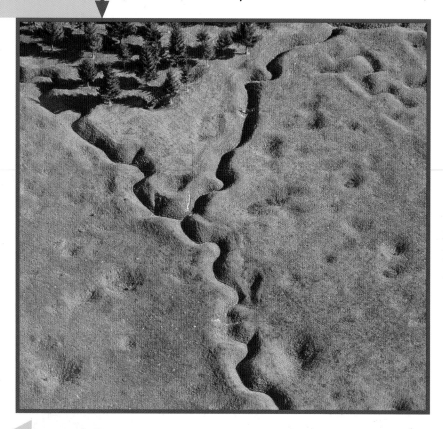

### Trench networks

Trenches were usually built in three or more connected lines, with a front line trench and two or more support trenches behind it. Behind these would be **artillery** positions. Communication trenches connected them, so soldiers could move between trenches with a lower risk of being killed by **sniper** or **shell** fire.

Standing before the **front line** trench would be dense rows of barbed wire, often laid in thick, tubular tiers. As defensive techniques grew more advanced, lines of barbed wire would be arranged with deliberate gaps or weak spots. In this way, approaching **infantrymen** could be herded into a 'killing ground', where machine gun fire would be at its most concentrated.

## New techniques

Later in the war, German trenches, and then Allied ones, were arranged with greater sophistication. Instead of a continuous front line trench, there was a series of small outposts intended to slow down attacking infantry. Behind this was a battlezone full of **strongpoints**. Even further back was a line of artillery and machine gun nests. Such deep defences were even more difficult to attack than the previous lines of trenches.

*Barbed wire was invented in 1873 and originally used to replace wooden fencing around grazing land for cattle in the American West. Employed here to protect French troops in their trench, barbed wire proved to be a deadly hindrance to attacking troops.*

## Forts

Not all of the Western Front was defended by trenches. In some parts of the line, especially at the French strongpoint of Verdun and the German Hindenburg Line, there were huge, concrete forts. Such fortifications were built to withstand heavy bombardment.

Verdun became the scene of some of the worst fighting of the war. Over a ten-month campaign from February to December 1916, German troops overran Fort Douaumont there, and forced the defenders of Fort Vaux to surrender for lack of water. But the French were grimly determined to hold on to their fortresses. In the end the Verdun campaign ground to a halt, with losses of around a third of a million men on both sides.

# Life in the trenches

The experience of being in the **front line** trenches was so exhausting and terrifying that soldiers were rarely stationed there for more than a week. In any given month, a soldier may also have spent a week in a support trench and two weeks at the rear.

## Keeping busy

In the lulls between big battles, there was still constant activity in the trenches. By day, any soldier who showed himself above the trench **parapet** risked instant death, so **periscopes** were often used to keep a watch on enemy activity. These crude wooden boxes were about two-thirds of a metre long, had a reflecting mirror at each end, and saved many lives.

*A US Marine receives first aid treatment for his wounds. In the insanitary conditions of the trenches, it was hard to prevent wounds from becoming infected.*

Darkness offered greater protection. At night, men set out into no man's land or to the **shell**-pocked craters around their own trenches. There they repaired gaps in barbed wire or fixed field telephone lines. Sometimes small groups would venture towards enemy lines to check their strength or carry out hit-and-run raids.

*We are fairly plagued by rats. They have eaten nearly everything in the mess, including the tablecloth and the operations orders! We borrowed a large cat and shut it up at night to exterminate them, and found the place empty next morning. The rats must have eaten it up, bones, fur, and all, and dragged it to their holes.*

P H Pilditch, British officer at Ypres, France.

# Home comforts and trench horrors

Men in the trenches were generally well fed and often able to bring some home comforts with them. There was even a postal service so regular and efficient that cakes and other perishable food could be sent to soldiers from home.

However, most trenches were miserable places. They needed considerable upkeep, and even this was often not enough to keep them from flooding in the soggy landscape and dreary climate of northern Europe. In winter, rain turned everything to mud. Trenches would sometimes flood to waist level, and soldiers often suffered from a form of frost-bite called trench foot. In summer, the heat and flies made the stench of **latrines** and dead bodies unbearable. Huge rats fed on the corpses of men and horses, and soldiers tried to keep their numbers down by shooting or beating them to death.

*[It was]…an underground dwelling approached by forty steps hewn into the solid chalk, so that even the heaviest shells at this depth made no more than a pleasant rumble…. In one wall I had a bed hewn out…at its head hung an electric light so I could read. The whole was shut off from the outer world by a dark-red curtain with rod and rings.*

German soldier Ernst Junger describing the living quarters in his trench on the Western Front.

*In their well-built trench on the Western Front in 1915, German soldiers search their clothes for signs of lice. Most men had their hair cropped as closely as possible to their skull to make delousing easier.*

Illness and **infestation** spread like wildfire in the trenches. Everyone became plagued by lice within a day or two of front line duty. Not only did they cause maddening itching, but lice transmitted a debilitating sickness known as trench fever.

Generally, French and British trenches were particularly squalid. This was partly due to the Allied leaders' belief that the trenches were temporary, and the war would once again become one of movement. German trenches were on the whole much better built and kept. German commanders recognized the permanency of the trenches far sooner, and their men lived in much greater safety and comfort.

# Uniforms, rifles and bayonets

## Protective clothing

For several hundred years before World War One, many armies had worn bright, colourful uniforms. Such outfits clearly identified the wearer, especially in the terror and confusion of hand-to-hand fighting. Uniforms also enabled commanders overlooking a battle to have a clear idea of where their troops were. But by the early 20th century, such conspicuous outfits were looking increasingly out of place. Most armies were issued with duller fabrics, all the better to conceal them from their enemies.

Even in 1914, French soldiers still wore blue tunics and bright red trousers, and regarded their German enemy's drab field-grey uniforms with disdain. The British army wore khaki, although Scottish regiments were allowed to wear tartan kilts. But as the war dragged on, the French discarded their bright costumes, and even the Scots took to covering their kilts with a khaki outer skirt. The penny had finally dropped: the less a man could be seen, the less likely he was to be shot.

*The soldiers who fought in World War One were as varied as their uniforms, but most carried rifles. This group of irregular soldiers from Bulgaria fought on the Balkan Front. Bulgaria was allied to the Central Powers and invaded Serbia in 1915.*

Soft peaked caps were also replaced with heavy metal helmets during the course of the war. Despite their obvious use in protecting a soldier's head from **shell** and **shrapnel** fragments, helmets were not popular with everyone as they were uncomfortable to wear.

## Infantry weapons

The main weapon for all **infantry** in the war was the **rifle**. The Germans, for example, had the Mauser Gewehr 98; the British had the 1907 Lee-Enfield; and the Americans the M1903 Springfield. All these weapons were of similar type and quality. They all had a bolt action, which meant the user pulled back a bolt in the rifle to clear one **round** from the firing chamber and load a fresh one. They all had **magazines**, which allowed the user to fire off several shots rapidly, without the need to reload. They were all accurate to at least 550 metres, but could fire a bullet over 3200 metres.

## The spirit of the bayonet

When an infantryman went into battle, he attached a **bayonet** to the end of his rifle to turn it, in effect, into a spear. Different armies had their own distinctive bayonet. The British had a knife blade type, the French had a thin needle type (which broke all too easily) and the Germans had a blade with a serrated edge.

Instructors talked about 'the spirit of the bayonet', meaning the courage and determination a soldier should show in killing his enemy by the terribly intimate method of stabbing him. Soldiers were told that their enemies had a particular fear of the bayonet (as if any man wouldn't), and that its enthusiastic use gave them a psychological advantage over their foe.

*A French corporal suddenly stood before me, both our bayonets at the ready, he to kill me, I to kill him. Pushing his weapon aside I stabbed him in the chest. He dropped his rifle and fell.... I stood over him for a few seconds and then I gave him the* coup de grâce *[meaning 'finishing stroke']. After we had taken the enemy position, I felt giddy, my knees shook, and I was actually sick.*

German army corporal Stephan Westman describing hand-to-hand fighting.

*American soldiers fire rifles at the enemy from their trench in France in 1918. Their rifles were equipped with bayonets for use in hand-to-hand fighting, especially when there was a risk of hitting their own side with rifle fire.*

13

# Other weapons of trench warfare

### Grenades

Grenades had been used effectively in the Russo-Japanese War and were enthusiastically taken up by the German army in World War One. They were little metal cases packed with explosives, light enough to be thrown by a man. There were two basic types. German troops mostly used ones which looked like a metal **canister** on a stick, such as the Stielhandgranate. The British and French used smaller round or oval-shaped grenades, such as the Mills bomb.

Some grenades were designed to explode on impact, but most had a timed **fuse** of around five seconds. Using them required great skill and courage. Thrown too soon, they could be caught and thrown back, and the act of throwing often exposed a grenadier (grenade-throwing soldier) to enemy fire.

The British and French armies were much slower than the Germans in introducing grenades. To compensate for this, Allied troops took to making their own by packing explosives, nails and scrap metal into empty tin cans. Grenades were tremendously effective, and eventually became the favoured weapon of **infantrymen** in trench warfare.

### Field mortars

Once the war had settled into a stalemate, another new weapon was introduced: the tube-like field mortar. A kind of portable, miniature **howitzer**, a mortar such as the British Stokes was light enough to be carried by a small team of men. One French mortar, the Crapouillot, was light enough to be carried on a man's back.

Mortars were immensely useful. Firing almost straight into the air, in a near vertical **trajectory**, they could deliver high explosives, **shrapnel**, smoke bombs and even poison gas **shells** from one trench to another.

## Flame-throwers

One of the most terrible trench weapons was the flame-thrower, which used pressurized gas from a canister to project a mixture of burning oil and petrol. Although devices that projected fire had been used from ancient times, the flame-thrower as we know it today was invented in Germany in 1906. The idea was also adopted by both the British and French armies.

Heavy flame-throwers, such as the British Livens, were installed in some trenches, but were impractical. They used vast amounts of precious fuel and were too cumbersome to be moved effectively. Much more useful were portable flame-throwers with smaller gas canisters, such as the German Kleif and Wex, and the French Schilt. These were light enough to be carried by one man and could be employed in enemy trenches, where they were murderously effective.

*A German assault force attacks using flame-throwers. The job of flame-thrower operator required a special kind of courage. He would be a priority target for enemy troops, and his own highly inflammable load could easily explode, enveloping him with burning fuel.*

## Mines

One type of warfare on the Western Front was the digging of mines, or underground tunnels, from one trench to another. Army construction workers were put to work digging underneath the enemy front line. Many of the tunnel diggers had previously been coal miners or had dug tunnels for underground rail networks in Europe's capitals. Huge amounts of explosives were then planted at the end of the tunnel. There were many dangers involved in this work, and the fear of being buried alive in a collapsing tunnel was always present. Also, the enemy would sometimes burrow into these tunnels, and miners faced the terrifying prospect of fighting underground gun battles.

It took the Allies two years to dig the tunnels that reached under the German trenches at Messines in France. There, 500 tonnes of explosives were **detonated** on 7 June 1917. The sound of the explosion could be heard in central London several hundred kilometres away.

# Machine guns

Aside from the squalor of the trenches, no other image seems to symbolize World War One so starkly as that of the machine gun. Perched atop a trench **parapet** and worked by two or more men, it spat a lethal ribbon of bullets at attacking troops. **Artillery** killed more soldiers overall, but these were deaths caused by **shells** fired from far behind the lines. The contact between a machine gunner and his victims was much more immediate and personal.

## An efficient killing machine

With an average rate of fire of around 600 **rounds** a minute, the machine gun could kill more efficiently than any other weapon of the time. On the first day of the Battle of the Somme on the Western Front in 1916, German machine guns cut down 60,000 British soldiers. Machine guns also proved invaluable in battles on other fronts. In 1914, at Tannenburg (in what is now Poland) on the Eastern Front, German gunners massacred the advancing Russian army. At Gallipoli (in present-day Turkey), Australian and New Zealand units were devastated by Turkish gunners in 1915.

*A French machine gun crew is poised for action with their Hotchkiss machine gun in 1915. The Hotchkiss was one of the principal machine guns used in World War One.*

## Machine gun crews

The main machine guns used in the war – the German Maxim MG '08, the British Vickers Mk 1, the French Hotchkiss, the Russian Sokolov and the American Browning – were fairly standard in their performance. Their individual effectiveness depended very much on the skill of the crews that operated them.

Each gun usually had a team of around six men to operate it. One would fire as a second would carefully feed in the bullets, which were held in a metal or fabric strip. Two other men would keep them supplied with **ammunition**. This pair also kept the barrel of the gun cool in a water jacket so that it wouldn't overheat and stop working. Another two men would act as scouts. They doubled as personal guards for the gunner, who could expect no mercy if he fell into the hands of attacking troops.

## Pre-war development

The machine gun was developed during the late 19th century by American Hiram Maxim. It first earned its fearsome reputation in small-scale **colonial** wars between European powers and African and Asian countries. By the time World War One broke out, French military planners reckoned one machine gun was as effective as 150 or even 200 riflemen.

## Lighter weapons

At the start of World War One, most machine guns were very heavy, which restricted their use to trench defence. But their effectiveness encouraged the development of more portable machine guns, such as the German Madsen and British Lewis gun.

By the end of the war, the Germans had developed the first sub-machine gun, the Bergmann MP18. This could be carried by a single **infantryman**, and could fire 540 rounds a minute, almost as much as a heavy machine gun. The gunner had to be careful how he used it, however. The drum that carried its bullets only held 32 rounds, which could be fired off in less than four seconds.

*By the time United States soldiers entered World War One in 1917, smaller machine guns were being developed. These were light enough for their crews to carry them into battle alongside attacking infantrymen.*

# The power of artillery

## Major offensive weapon

Soldiers had good reason to fear **artillery**. These were the large guns that fired **shells**, which are metal cases of various shapes containing explosives or other lethal materials. Over 70 per cent of all **casualties** in World War One were caused by shell fire. One German statistic estimated that artillery killed fourteen of the enemy for every one killed by **infantry**. Yet this killing power was bought at a massive material cost. Other statistics from the war suggest that more than 1,000 shells were used for every actual death by artillery.

Until the arrival of the tank, artillery was the major offensive weapon of World War One. It was artillery shells that created the treeless and cratered landscape of no man's land. Artillery took up an immense part of most armies' resources and effort. By the end of the war the British army, for example, had half a million soldiers in its artillery units. On the home front 70 per cent of all British factory workers were employed in the **munitions** industry.

## New developments

Most armies' artillery units used highly efficient weapons, although the Russian army occasionally used guns that dated back to the Crimean War of 1853–56. By the time of World War One, guns were generally breech-loaded, meaning that shells were placed in the back and fired out of the front. This system was more efficient than that of the old muzzle-loaded artillery.

These guns also had **barrel**-only recoil. This meant a mechanism in the gun allowed only the barrel to move back (recoil) when the shell fired. The rest of

*British soldiers fire 20-cm howitzers during the Battle of the Somme in 1916. Artillery bombardments were lethally effective. In the Battle of the Somme, well over a million soldiers were killed in four months, and this high death rate was due in large part to new and powerful artillery.*

the gun stayed in exactly the same position. Guns such as this did not need to be re-aimed after every firing.

## Deadly shells

The effect of these developments was that a trained crew could fire 15 or more heavy shells a minute. The shells used in World War One were filled mostly with one of three materials. High explosives would usually **detonate** on impact. **Shrapnel** shells had a time **fuse**, which would usually detonate when the shell was in mid-air, raining down lethal metal balls on enemy soldiers below. By the end of the war, more than a quarter of all shells fired by artillery contained poisonous gas rather than explosives.

*French troops under shell fire at the Battle of Verdun in 1916. Millions of shells were fired during the ten-month battle.*

## Artillery weapons

There were several types of artillery weapons. These are the main ones:

**Artillery guns** fired low **trajectory**, high velocity shells over a long range. They were usually of two types: the field gun and the heavy gun. Field guns, such as the French 1897 75 mm and British Mk 1 18-pounder, were the lighter type and employed nearer to the **front line**. Heavy guns, such as the German 17 cm and French 220 mm Schneider, were difficult to move. But they were more effective, especially against deep **bunkers** and concrete **fortifications**.

**Howitzers**, including guns such as the French Schneider 520 mm and the German Big Bertha 42 cm, fired heavy shells on a high, short range trajectory. The shells arrived with a terrifying whistle, but at least that gave warning of their approach.

**Siege guns**, such as the German Paris gun, were huge weapons usually mounted on rails. They could fire a 90-kg shell over 110 km (68 mi), and a few were used to attack the French capital of Paris from behind German lines. Accuracy declined rapidly after the first 20 shells, so the barrel had to be replaced regularly.

# Using the new artillery

World War One generals were forced to place their highly-skilled and valuable **artillery** crews out of range of enemy **rifle** fire. Away from the **front line**, it was difficult to fire artillery with full effectiveness. Artillery commanders had to rely on spotters who could observe where

the **shells** were landing and then relay the information via field telephone or even **semaphore**. Later in the war, aerial spotters would radio this information from above the action. Generally, the solution was to fire more shells to compensate for lack of accuracy caused by distance.

The military planners had great hopes for their sophisticated artillery weapons. They hoped they would break through enemy barbed wire, which proved so effective in stopping soldiers advancing. But barbed wire was curiously invulnerable to shell blast. Shots that landed in the wire-strewn 'killing zone' in front of the front line blew a crater in the ground, but the wire would simply fall back unbroken into it.

*A shell is fired with a huge blast by an Allied 36-cm artillery gun in Argonne, France. The shell could travel 48 km (30 mi) to German positions. But it was hard to know exactly where it would land.*

## Creeping barrages

It was also hoped that artillery would be able to protect soldiers as they advanced towards enemy trenches. A 'creeping **barrage**' would be laid down, where shells would fall in front of the troops, slowly moving forward across no man's land. But in the days before effective radio communication, it was impossible to delay a barrage if troops became bogged down or caught in enemy fire before they reached the best position behind the curtain of shell fire.

## Gun positions

Artillery units did their best to camouflage their positions, and guns were placed so that if one was hit, exploding **ammunition** would not destroy other guns around it. Concealment became much more difficult with the arrival of **reconnaissance** planes. The Germans became expert at dropping gas shells onto French and British artillery positions.

## Making munitions

On the home fronts of the fighting nations, the need for vast numbers of shells put great demands on both production and transport systems. A British navy **blockade** cut German supplies of nitrates, essential ingredients for high explosives. German chemist Fritz Haber developed a process whereby nitrates were extracted from atmospheric nitrogen (quite literally out of the air!) and Germany was able to continue with shell production.

To make up the numbers of workers needed, women were encouraged to take positions in **munitions** factories. Many thousands joined the workplace in manufacturing jobs that had previously been reserved for men. Earning good money, and enjoying the freedom an independent income provided, was a novel experience for many women.

*Women in World War One factories proved themselves to be productive and efficient workers, much to the surprise of men, who thought women were incapable of such industrial tasks.*

*Dear Wilhelm,*
*I send you greetings from my grave in the earth. We shall soon become mad with this awful artillery fire. Day and night it goes on without ceasing. We sit all day deep down in the earth, with neither light nor sunshine, just waiting for death, which may reach us any moment.*

Letter home from a German soldier of the Third Magdeburg Regiment, in a trench on the Western Front, Autumn 1916.

Even if the gas did not directly harm the gun crews, the tricky business of loading and firing their guns was made much more difficult when wearing gas masks.

Yet for all its fearsome killing power, artillery was never truly able to do what it was supposed to do: bombard enemy trenches and barbed wire into such a pulp that advancing troops would meet no resistance. Trenches, especially German ones, were just too well built to be destroyed by simple explosives.

# Poisonous gas

### A new weapon

Poisonous gas was one of the few completely new types of weapons used in World War One. It rarely killed its victims: a mere three per cent of gas **casualties** actually died on the battlefield. But it was so effective at disabling troops that by 1918, about 25 per cent of British **shells** and 80 per cent of German shells carried gas instead of high explosives.

The Germans, at the time world leaders in chemical science, were the first to use gas as a weapon. In January 1915, they released poison gas from **canisters** at Bolimov on the Eastern Front. Strong winds and wet weather made this first use ineffective, but when gas was unleashed in more favourable conditions on the Western Front, it caused dreadful panic in Allied trenches. France and Britain **retaliated** with their own gas attacks shortly afterwards.

## Types of gas

The first gas to be used was chlorine. It caused choking and vomiting, and could be fatal if inhaled in sufficient quantity. Phosgene followed within the year, and produced similar symptoms. Like chlorine, it could be released from canisters placed on the front line, but it could also be carried in shells.

Deadliest of all was dichlorethylsulphide, known as mustard gas. It was introduced in 1917. Carried mainly by shells, it would linger where it fell for days. Anyone who came into contact with it would suffer blistered and burned skin and lungs, and often blindness, followed by a slow, choking death by pneumonia. Other gases were only effective when inhaled, but mustard gas attacked the skin and would penetrate through uniforms to do its horrible work. Its low battlefield kill rate disguised the fact that many gas victims would be crippled for life, or die lingering deaths in the years following the war.

## No advantage

Gas had disadvantages as a weapon. A strong wind could blow it back to the very men who had released it, and in wet weather it would gather uselessly at ankle level. Fighting for both attacker and defender was much more difficult in the protective clothing both sides were forced to wear. Gas gave neither side in the war an advantage, and just made life at the **front line** even more horrible for everyone concerned.

As use of poison gas became widespread, measures against it improved. At first, goggles and chemical-soaked mouth pads were issued to troops. Later, hoods and then facemasks with air filters were developed, for both people and horses!

## Gas attack

British war poet Wilfred Owen captured the horror of a gas attack in one of his most famous poems, *Dulce et Decorum Est*, meaning 'it is sweet and honourable'. (The rest of this Latin phrase is *pro patria mori*, meaning 'to die for one's country'.) The poem depicts exhausted troops trudging away from the front line *drunk with fatigue; deaf even to the hoots of gas-shells dropping softly behind.*

Owen then describes the terror of the actual attack:

*Gas! Gas! Quick, boys! – An ecstasy of fumbling,*
*Fitting the clumsy helmets just in time,*
*But someone still was yelling out and stumbling...*
*Dim through the misty panes and thick green light,*
*As under a green sea, I saw him drowning.*

*In all my dreams, before my helpless sight,*
*He plunges at me, guttering, choking, drowning.*

Finally, he tells of the awful after-effects the gas has on its luckless victim:

*...watch the white eyes writhing in his face,*
*His hanging face, like a devil's sick of sin;*
*If you could hear, at every jolt, the blood*
*Come gargling from his froth-corrupted lungs,*
*Obscene as cancer, bitter as the cud*
*Of vile, incurable sores on innocent tongues...*

# Transport

The first motor car took to the road in 1886, nearly 30 years before the outbreak of World War One. But modern armies were slow to make use of motorized transport, and most continued to make heavy use of horse-drawn vehicles throughout the war.

## Railway travel

The armies of World War One also relied on trains, both to move them near to the fighting, and to keep them supplied at the front. In Germany, the railway system had been constructed with a view to moving troops speedily to the nation's borders.

On the Western Front, and on the German side of the Eastern Front, railway lines functioned efficiently throughout the war. Standard gauge steam engines – those that ran on tracks 143.5 centimetres wide – would pull their wagons to railheads behind the front lines. Here, troops and supplies would be dropped and continue to the front by other vehicles or on foot. There were also light railways constructed to take supplies from the railhead to just behind the front. These had a smaller gauge track (60 centimetres) that was much easier and cheaper to build than the ordinary standard gauge.

## Motor vehicles

Motorized vehicles designed for other purposes were used at the front. Parisian taxis ferried thousands of French soldiers out to fight the Germans in the first frantic weeks of the war. By the time the war ended, motorized lorries, staff cars, and especially ambulances, were increasingly joining horse-drawn vehicles at the front.

## Essential supplies

As the war lengthened from months to years, good transport was essential for a constant supply of **munitions**, food and **reinforcements**. When French soldiers were fighting desperately to hold on to Verdun (see page 9), one small country road saw supply-packed motor vehicles

*Before the days of widespread motorized transport, the military relied on dogs as well as horses to move equipment. This team of dogs is on its way to the front with the Belgian army, pulling a machine gun.*

pass every fourteen seconds on their way to the front line. The road was dubbed the *Voie Sacrée* (Sacred Way).

In Russia, the most **technologically** backward of all the major fighting nations, it was another story. Russian troops suffered terribly because their transport system was poor. A hurried programme of factory building had enabled them to produce arms and **ammunition** on a level close to that of Germany, France and Britain. But the Russians were unable to keep their armies supplied with these weapons. This meant that Russian soldiers often went into battle unarmed, with orders to pick up a **rifle** and ammunition from a fallen comrade during the battle. Such poor planning over transport contributed greatly to the number of mutinies among Russian soldiers.

## Marching off to war

For many soldiers, the surest way to travel was to march. All generals had calculating tables telling them how quickly a set number of troops could march from one area to another, and usually assumed a speed of 4 to 5 km (2.5 to 3 mi) per hour, including breaks for resting.

Moving troops in this way had changed little since Roman times, but now there were modern hazards to contend with. Closely packed troops were vulnerable to both **shell** fire and aerial attacks. **Reconnaissance** planes could spot long columns of marching men all too easily. Where possible, troops marched close to walls, trees or buildings, so the shadow they cast could not be seen from the air.

*Buses were sometimes commandeered from Paris or London and stuffed with shells and supplies. They would be seen trundling down muddy roads near to the front lines. This London double-decker bus was converted for army use with the addition of **artillery** and wooden siding.*

# Tanks

The tank was the most important **innovation** of World War One. The first tanks of the war look hopelessly clumsy and somehow comical compared to the sleek, high-tech war machines we know today. But a picture of a tank can never convey the terror that these lumbering monsters inspired, grinding over no man's land, spitting fire from their armoured sides, and causing **front line** troops to flee in fear of being crushed under their clanking tracks. They could thunder across trenches and crush barbed wire, all the while spraying enemy soldiers with machine gun fire or high explosive **shells**.

## The first tank

The name for a tank came about during the weapon's development, and was intended to make the enemy think these vehicles were mobile water tanks. Initially described by the British as 'machine gun destroyers', the word tank stuck.

*This illustration by Stanley L Wood shows a British tank, the Mark I, used in warfare for the first time at the Battle of the Somme. The German soldiers with their rifles and grenades stood little chance of defending themselves.*

Lord Kitchener, one of Britain's leading generals in the early part of the war, dismissed the tank as a 'pretty mechanical toy'. Fortunately other British commanders disagreed and the new weapon went into production. The first fighting tank was the Mark I, developed by a British team under Lt-Colonel Ernest Swinton in 1915. Its **caterpillar tracks** were much better at crossing difficult terrain than wheels. France also produced a successful tank, the Renault FT17, soon after the British.

## First use in battle

Tanks were first used in battle at the Somme in France on 15 September 1916, when a squadron of 49 tanks was deployed. Eighteen reached the enemy trenches and were immensely effective. But the fact that 31 tanks had broken down or got stuck in the mud on the way completely overshadowed their success.

A year later, tanks had another chance to prove their worth. In November 1917, at Cambrai in France, 378 Allied tanks advanced on a 12-kilometre (7.5-mile) front. It was here the tank's reputation as an invaluable **offensive** weapon was sealed. Earlier that year, 400,000 men had been killed in a terrible three-month massacre at Passchendaele in Belgium. It was a high price to pay for the advance of a small section of the Allied front line by only 9 kilometres (5.5 miles). At Cambrai, the 378 tanks and their attendant **infantry** advanced the same distance in a single day.

Americans were quick to seize on the tank's potential. During World War One they used British and French tanks in their own armoured divisions. The Germans used captured Allied tanks when they could, but had only produced 20 of their own huge A7V tanks before the end of the war. Other principal fighting nations, such as Russia and Italy, had just started making tanks when the war came to an end.

*World War One tanks, such as this British Mark IV, were slow, moving at no more than 7 km (4.3 mi) per hour, but they could climb a steep slope and cross a 2.5 m trench with their caterpillar tracks.*

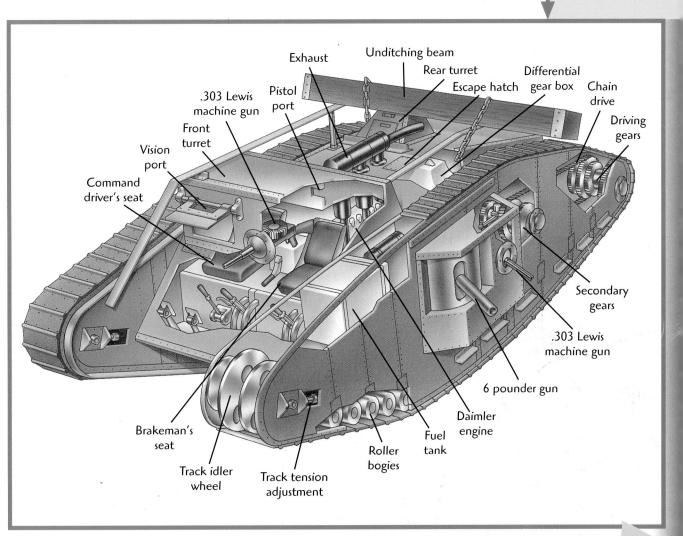

Exhaust · Unditching beam · Rear turret · Differential gear box · Chain drive · Escape hatch · Driving gears · .303 Lewis machine gun · Pistol port · Front turret · Vision port · Command driver's seat · Secondary gears · .303 Lewis machine gun · 6 pounder gun · Daimler engine · Fuel tank · Roller bogies · Brakeman's seat · Track idler wheel · Track tension adjustment

# Mighty warships

*A battleship fires its guns in a scene from the* Battle of Jutland *painted by Winston McGoran.*

## Supremacy at sea

The navies of Britain and Germany had engaged in a vastly expensive arms race before World War One. They built huge battleships called dreadnoughts in a bid to outdo each other as naval powers. At the outbreak of the war, Britain was still way ahead, with 21 dreadnoughts to Germany's 13.

The British navy had been the most powerful in the world for more than a century. In this period, there had been great **technological** changes. Warships were now made of steel rather than wood and were driven by powerful steam **turbine engines**. Their **rifled** guns were held in moveable **turrets**. The explosive-packed **shells** they fired could be hurled over distances as much as 16 kilometres (10 miles). Thanks to intricate range-finding machinery, these shells often found their target with deadly accuracy.

Warships included several different types. Among them were cruisers, fast medium-sized ships; and destroyers, small warships used to protect larger ships from attack. Destroyers were well armed with huge guns and torpedoes. Battleships were the largest and most heavily armed warships, usually clad in immense **armour plating**. Dreadnoughts were the pride of any fleet. Named after the first of their kind, the British HMS *Dreadnought*, these giant battleships were a devastatingly effective combination of speed and fire power.

## The Battle of Jutland

Britain and Germany were both very reluctant to risk their fleets in an all out battle. The two navies met only once, at the Battle of Jutland in May 1916. During the battle, 6100 British and 2550 Germans were killed. Britain lost more ships (fourteen to Germany's nine), but her navy was still the most powerful in the world.

## Blockade tactics

When the war broke out, both sides used their navies to impose **blockades** on their enemies, to prevent them from importing goods from overseas. In previous wars, blockades had been close to enemy coastlines, but with explosive-packed mines a major threat, as well as accurate torpedoes, such closeness was now impossible. Instead, distant blockades were established.

Britain and France blocked German trade via the North Sea and the Mediterranean. The blockade proved effective. German citizens referred to the winter of 1916–17 as 'turnip winter' because food shortages were so acute that this home-grown vegetable became a staple part of the German diet. However, Germany and the Ottoman **Empire** imposed a successful blockade of their own on Russia in the Baltic and Black Seas.

Because of British naval power, the English Channel crossing between Britain and France was always open. Britain was able to import food and goods for its citizens and armies throughout the war. But Allied ships faced a much more serious threat from Germany's submarine fleet.

*Two battleship squadrons of the German navy rest in Kiel Harbour on the coast of Germany. After the Battle of Jutland in May 1916, German warships never left their harbours in force for the rest of the war.*

## Mines and torpedoes

Warships were faced with weapons such as the torpedo and mine. Like armoured battleships, mines and torpedoes were not strictly new to World War One, but both proved very effective.

Torpedoes were originally invented in the mid-19th century for ships, but became the principal weapon of submarines. They were missiles, launched through the water by ships or submarines to explode against the hull of an enemy ship. Powered by compressed air, they had a range of 9000 m.

Mines were as terrifying a prospect at sea as they were on land. Consisting of a case of explosives, they could be laid anywhere, ready to explode at the slightest disturbance. Unexploded mines in the water, as on land, continue to be lethal hazards long after wars are over.

# Submarines

Underwater war machines of one sort or another have been around since ancient Greek times. In more modern times, primitive submarines were used in the American War of Independence. But it was a series of gradual developments in the 19th century that turned what was first a novelty into a formidable fighting machine.

## Technological developments

Air-filled or water-filled ballast tanks, which raised or lowered a submarine in the water, were developed in the early 19th century. Torpedoes were invented in the 1860s. So was the **periscope**, a viewing device enabling a submarine crew to see above water and make an attack from below. Powerful electric motors were introduced in the 1880s. (Previous means of power, from oars to hand-turned propellers to steam engines, were hardly practical underwater.) And by the early 20th century, submarines were fitted with two engines: an electric one for underwater, and a cheaper, faster, air-guzzling diesel one for surface travel.

## Effective weapon

With all the **technology** in place, nations such as Britain, France and Germany began to add submarines to their navies. When war broke out, they proved immediately effective. One German submarine sank four British navy ships when the war was barely a month old. In 1915, a German torpedo sank a British passenger ship, the *Lusitania*. About 1200 were killed, including 128 US citizens, and this led more Americans to favour entering the war.

*German U-boats were dreaded by the Allies in World War One. They sank thousands of merchant and military ships. Yet for all their effectiveness, submarines were often coffins for their crews. Nearly half of all U-boat crews eventually went down with their submarine.*

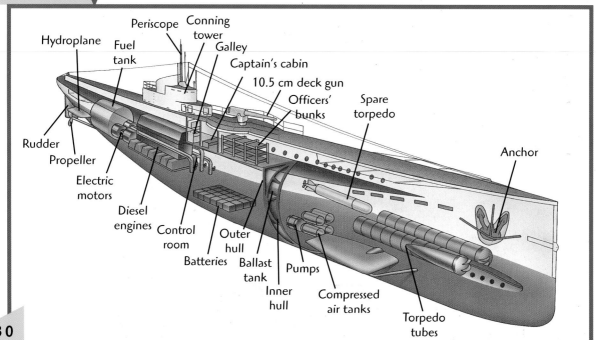

Hydroplane · Periscope · Conning tower · Galley · Captain's cabin · 10.5 cm deck gun · Officers' bunks · Spare torpedo · Anchor · Fuel tank · Rudder · Propeller · Electric motors · Diesel engines · Control room · Batteries · Outer hull · Ballast tank · Inner hull · Pumps · Compressed air tanks · Torpedo tubes

It was the submarine's use against merchant ships that was most effective. And it was Germany that devoted most attention and resources to developing a submarine fleet for this purpose. A **blockade** against the powerful British fleet on the surface was not possible. But one underwater nearly succeeded in starving Britain out of the war, as merchant ships full of vital supplies were sunk by U-boats.

*Two German sailors push a torpedo into the loading tube of a World War One U-boat, readying it for its next mission.*

The statistics prove the effectiveness of submarines, especially compared to other navy weapons. At the height of the sea war in 1917, German submarines sank 2439 Allied ships, compared to 234 sunk by German mines or surface ships. Altogether, German submarines sank nearly 5000 ships during the war. These figures are even more remarkable in the light of the fact that the German submarine fleet never numbered more than 140 vessels.

## Surface ships fight back

When dealing with isolated merchant ships, a submarine crew would often surface and use its guns, which was cheaper than using torpedoes. So small merchant vessels called Q-ships were introduced. Armed with hidden weapons, they were ready to sink U-boats that surfaced to attack them. In 1916, underwater listening devices called hydrophones were developed. These could detect submarines by the sound of their motors. Once found, the submarines were attacked with depth-charges, which were explosive-filled cylinders set to **detonate** at a certain depth. Anti-submarine **minefields** were also effective. In one anti-submarine minefield, 165,000 mines were laid across U-boat lanes in the North Sea and English Channel.

The most useful defence against submarines was the **convoy** system. Introduced in May 1917, at the height of German U-boat success, this tactic involved groups of cargo ships travelling together with a navy escort. This gave the U-boats just one chance to spot the ships rather than the repeated opportunities offered if they travelled separately. And if they did attack a convoy, the U-boat crew could be sure of **retaliation**.

# Aeroplanes

Following the Wright brothers' first powered flight in 1903, the pioneers of aviation were closely watched by military planners keen to make use of this marvellous new **technology**. Both the US and French armies bought aircraft designs from the Wright brothers in 1908.

When war broke out in 1914, the armies and navies of the main combat nations had their own aerial units, each with around 200 to 300 aircraft. To begin with it was thought that these planes would be used for **reconnaissance** and **artillery** spotting.

## Bombers

As the war progressed, however, other uses developed. Large, multi-engined aircraft – such as Russian Sikorskys, Italian Capronis and German Gothas – were built to carry bombs. Such aircraft could attack cities hundreds of kilometres behind the front lines, although they were never used in large enough numbers to cause significant damage.

*A British Sopwith Camel exchanges fire with German fighter planes above the Western Front. These aircraft were called biplanes because of their two sets of wings, one above the other.*

## Fighters

The most useful aircraft of all proved to be small, light and highly **manoeuvrable** fighter planes such as the French Nieuport, German Fokker and British Sopwith Camel. At the start of the war, enemy pilots fired at each other with pistols. Then heavy machine guns were fitted to cockpits, but they were clumsy and difficult to use. In 1915 the Fokker aircraft designers invented the synchronized machine gun. This had an interrupting mechanism, and could fire directly through the propeller blades at the front of the plane. It enabled a pilot to aim his weapon by lining up his aircraft behind his enemy.

## Multiple uses

By 1917 all sides were using aircraft for reconnaissance and ground attack, and as artillery spotters, bombers, and fighters. German planes, which attacked trenches in squadrons of up to 30 aircraft, were especially effective at harassing British and French troops.

Although the Germans generally had the most advanced aircraft, victory in the air war went to the nations that could produce the most aircraft. By 1918, Britain and France had won control of the skies. In the final battles of World War One, their aircraft played a major role in attacking German troops both at the front and behind it.

In the course of the war, the aeroplane had changed from a wondrous novelty to an essential fighting machine. On the Western Front alone, there were 10,000 combat planes. But the cost in lives was terrible. Germany and Britain lost 50 per cent of their pilots, France over 70 per cent. The majority of these men had been killed in accidents – either at the front or in training – which proved the dangers of introducing new, barely tried technology into such a central combat role.

## The first airforce

In Britain squabbles over resources for aircraft between the army and navy resulted in the formation of the Royal Air Force, the world's first independent airforce, in 1918. (Aerial units for other nations were part of the army or navy, and many still are to this day.)

## The flying aces

The arrival of the synchronized machine gun heralded the era of the flying ace. Men such as Robert Little of Australia, William Bishop of Canada, Eddie Rickenbacker of the United States and Mick Mannock of Britain became the war's most glamorous figures. In a war of inglorious mud and mass slaughter, they engaged in single combat like medieval knights, whirling and wheeling in a clear, blue sky. Their countries mourned them as national heroes if they were shot down.

*Most famous of the flying aces was German Baron von Richthofen, nicknamed 'the Red Baron', who shot down 80 enemy aircraft before he was killed in action in 1918. Richthofen commanded a unit called the 'Flying Circus'. He realized early on that the future of aerial combat lay in squadron **tactics** and teamwork.*

# Airships

To the **civilians** who lived in fear of their arrival, there was something deeply sinister about the German Zeppelin airships. These huge, lumbering beasts of the air—up to 650 feet (200 meters) long—would leave their bases at dusk, slip through the night sky to drop their bombs on cities, and then return before dawn. They were able to fly higher than the earliest fighter planes, but if an airplane pilot did locate one, he would be met by a hail of machine gun bullets from several of the airship's many gunners.

## Bomb carriers

The Germans were very proud of their airships, invented by and named after Count Ferdinand von Zeppelin. They represented an impressive technological achievement. Lifted into the air by huge quantities of hydrogen gas carried inside a lightweight steel skeleton, they were propelled along by four gasoline engines at a speed of nearly 60 miles (100 kilometers) per hour. Most importantly, they could carry nearly two tons of bombs, far more than any other flying machine at the start of the war. Great things were expected of the airship. If anything was going to carry the war to the cities of enemy nations, and destroy their factories and homes, it was the Zeppelin.

## Look out below

Zeppelin attacks by the German army were launched all over Europe, from Paris to Brest-Litovsk, and from Bucharest to Sevastopol. Navy Zeppelins concentrated on bombing Britain, in the hope of bringing the war to a speedy end by paralyzing British industry.

But the Zeppelin promised far more than it delivered. The first one to attack London, on May 31, 1915, dropped 89 **incendiary bombs** and

*This Zeppelin carries the words "Gott Strafe England," meaning "God punish England." It was a slogan of the Germans in World War I. Because of this, the English word "strafe" has come to mean to attack or bombard, especially with machine gun fire from low-flying aircraft.*

30 grenades on the capital's heavily populated East End. Yet only seven people were killed in the attack. Before the war, people had speculated that flying machines would bring large-scale destruction to enemy cities. But Zeppelin raids caused only minor damage.

## Vulnerable targets

Their lack of effectiveness was only one problem. As aircraft technology advanced rapidly, fighter planes were soon able to fly as high as Zeppelins. Pilots discovered that incendiary (burning) bullets were perfect for setting Zeppelins on fire—the hydrogen gas that made them float was highly flammable. When a Zeppelin caught fire, it would light up the sky around it as it enveloped its crew in a huge fireball.

Zeppelins were also notoriously vulnerable to bad weather. In their campaign against Britain, 53 out of 77 of these huge machines were destroyed by storms, enemy aircraft, and anti-aircraft fire before the German military called them off. Remaining Zeppelins were sent to the **Eastern Front,** where enemy aircraft were neither as numerous nor as effective. There, they ferried supplies to German troops and continued to make bombing raids.

*A Zeppelin is caught in searchlights during a night attack over Britain.*

## Observation balloons

Hydrogen balloons were first employed in the Napoleonic wars in the early nineteenth century. They were extremely useful observation platforms. It was their use in the American Civil War that first gave Count Ferdinand von Zeppelin the idea for his huge mobile airships.

In World War I, observation balloons were often placed right behind the **front lines.** These balloons were prime targets for enemy fighters, so they were surrounded by batteries of anti-aircraft guns. Observation crews had such a dangerous job that they were the only aerial combatants issued parachutes during the war.

# Communications

*Women at work in a British navy communications room. The woman on the left is using a radio and the woman on the right is operating a telephone switchboard.*

*On the Balkan Front, two Turkish soldiers operate a field telephone from their shelter, a hole in the ground known as a foxhole. Although the telephone allowed for immediate contact, it required long lengths of wire to be laid from one point to another.*

The **technology** of electrical communication was still new when World War One began: the first radio transmissions were made in 1896, and field telephones were not used until the Russo-Japanese War of 1904–05. Radio and field telephones and **telegraphs** were utilized where possible in World War One, but more often than not commanders had to resort to other methods. **Semaphore**, runners, highly visible rocket signals and even carrier pigeons were all employed to carry messages to their front line troops.

## Communication problems

The field telephone used an extended wire to connect **front line** command posts with headquarters behind the lines. The telephone was immensely useful because it allowed for actual conversation, unlike the field telegraph. The field telegraph could only transmit messages in Morse code, a series of short or longer bleeps which correspond to the letters of the alphabet.

Transmitting Morse code messages under the stress of battle or bombardment was extremely difficult, however. And the wires for both telephone and telegraph were all too vulnerable to **shell** fire and other damage. Repairing them could be immensely dangerous. All sides knew how valuable these communication links were, and a man sent to an exposed spot to repair a broken line was a prime target for enemy **sniper** fire.

To compensate for this lack of effective communication, generals would often issue broad directives in advance to front line officers. But both generals and officers were unable to react sufficiently quickly when circumstances changed in the course of battle.

## Early use of radio

Radio, a form of communication without wires, was increasingly used in World War One. But it had its disadvantages. Early radio sets were clumsy, fragile devices that were easily damaged. Radio signals could also be picked up by the other side. In 1914 the German army monitored Russian radio signals before the Battle of Tannenburg on the Eastern Front. This told them exactly what the Russians planned to do.

Secret codes were used, but they could be cracked, especially if code books fell into the hands of the enemy. Throughout the war the British navy always knew what the German navy planned to do because the British had a code book found on the body of a drowned German naval officer early in the war. Also, as radio use became more frequent, so did the jamming, or blocking, of radio signals. This was done by transmitting another noise that made the original signal impossible to hear.

*This vehicle was used by the French as a mobile unit for carrier pigeons. The birds were trained to go to one particular location and then return. They carried messages tied to their legs.*

# Medicine

More than twelve million men were wounded in World War I. Injuries from bullets and **shells** were familiar to medical officers, but the scale of the ongoing fighting often made treatment difficult.

## Fighting infection and disease

On the **Western Front,** wounds rapidly became contaminated in the mud and squalor of the trenches. Antiseptics—chemicals used to keep wounds clean—were just not strong enough for the terrible infections and **gangrene** that resulted. Surgeons had to cut out the infection, and often had to remove an infected limb completely.

On the **Eastern Front,** disease was far more of a problem. There, a wounded man, his body struggling to stay alive already, was an easy target for any current **epidemic.** Millions of people died from diseases because there were no antibiotics to fight them.

*Emergency care took place wherever it was needed, and field hospitals sprang up behind the front lines. The ruins of this bombed church in France provided shelter for the wounded and medical staff.*

## Gas casualties

Poison gas was a new challenge to doctors and nurses. Treatment was crude: cough medicines and the inhaling of medicinal vapors (steam) were used to ease damaged lungs. Doctors also used these to try and stop the accumulation of fluids in the lungs that would slowly drown a man from the inside. Gas also caused a hideous form of infection in wounds known as gas gangrene. This was treated to an extent with injections to fight the poison, but again, the surgeons often had no choice but to cut out infected flesh.

## Helping the wounded

Dealing with wounds was a difficult task on the battlefront, but technology provided doctors with new tools for their patients. Portable X-ray machines, first used in 1898, allowed surgeons to locate bullets and shell fragments inside a wounded man. The discovery of the four main blood groups had been completed by 1900. This knowledge made blood **transfusions** much safer, and medical stations commonly kept supplies of blood available.

**Artillery** fire killed more men than any other weapon of the war, and also caused appalling injuries, particularly loss of limbs. A huge number of men lost arms and legs, encouraging the development of more realistic and effective artificial limbs.

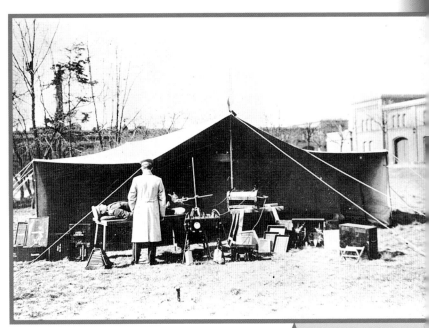

*A wounded German soldier is X-rayed in a tent in 1916.*

## Plastic surgery

Facial injuries were particularly common in the trenches, since the head was the most exposed part of the body. Therefore, the science of plastic surgery came of age during World War I. Surgeons presented with a wide array of disfiguring facial wounds made great advances in restoring the features of injured soldiers. New techniques, such as skin and bone grafts, were developed. So were procedures for wiring together a shattered jaw. Missing bits of facial bone, vital to restore a person's appearance, were replaced by internal rubber splints. One pioneer of plastic surgery, Dr. Harold Gillies of New Zealand, dealt with 2,000 facial injuries during the Battle of the Somme alone.

## Shell shock

A newly recognized medical condition of World War I was shell shock, an all-purpose description for **psychological** breakdown. Shell shock was a particular problem on the Western Front, because men were exposed to danger over such a prolonged period.

Soldiers suffering from shell shock might have no physical wounds but might shake uncontrollably, be paralyzed, or have no control over their bowels and bladders. **Front line** medical staff and officers were suspicious and were often quick to dismiss this condition. But the idea that wounds of the mind were just as real as wounds of the body gradually became accepted. Treatment varied from patience and sympathy to the use of electric shocks, and many victims were sent to psychiatric hospitals. Perhaps a quarter of a million men who fought in Europe suffered from shell shock.

# The cost of the war

World War One came to an end in 1918. One by one, Germany's allies had surrendered and Germany finally signed an **armistice** with the Allies on 11 November.

One German **front line** doctor described World War One despairingly as 'the suicide of nations'. So many young men were killed that it became fashionable to talk of the 'lost generation'. About 70 million men had been called to arms over the duration of the war. Of these, 37.5 million had been killed, wounded or taken prisoner. The actual death toll was around nine million, so around one in eight of those who served had died. Nine million **civilians** died too, mostly from starvation and disease in the Eastern theatres of the war.

## Civilians to soldiers

What was so shocking about these losses, aside from their number, was that most of the dead had been civilians before the war: Russian farm hands, German factory workers, French peasants, British clerks and Canadian school teachers. The war reached out its deadly fingers, plucked young men from their everyday lives, and destroyed them.

*Thousands of miles from home, a brave Australian soldier carries his wounded comrade to hospital in 1915, in what is now Turkey. Young men from all over the world became part of the lost generation.*

| TROOPS KILLED IN WORLD WAR ONE | |
|---|---|
| AUSTRALIA | 62,000 |
| AUSTRIA-HUNGARY | 922,000 |
| BRITAIN | 888,000 |
| CANADA | 65,000 |
| FRANCE | 1,300,000 |
| GERMANY | 1,800,000 |
| ITALY | 460,000 |
| NEW ZEALAND | 18,000 |
| OTTOMAN EMPIRE | 700,000 |
| RUSSIA | 1,700,000 |
| USA | 112,400 |

The death toll on the Western Front was astronomical, but even more soldiers and civilians perished on the Eastern Front. Such was the grisly scale of the slaughter that, on average, between five and six thousand people died for every day of the war's four terrible years.

## Other costs of the war

The bald statistics of dead and wounded give only one aspect of the human cost of World War One. The men who died left widows and fatherless children. The maimed and **shell** shocked, some reduced to begging in the street, others cared for by families or hidden in nursing homes and asylums, slowly faded away over the decades that followed. Many of the female half of the lost generation never married, whether from a simple lack of available men after the war, or from loyalty to those who had died.

## Memorials

Memorials to the fallen of World War One can be found in churchyards and village squares all over Europe. Huge monuments and burial grounds mark major battlefields. In northern France for example, where most of the fighting on the Western Front took place, tourists or pilgrims can visit cemeteries with mile upon mile of marble crosses. Many graves have names to record the final resting place for victims of what British Prime Minister Lloyd George called 'the ghastly butchery of vain and insane **offensives**'. Among those buried are those whose shattered remains prevented any accurate identification. Their gravestones are marked 'known unto God'.

Rows of crosses at a military cemetery in France mark the graves of World War One soldiers. Most who died were under 30 years old, and many were not yet out of their teens.

# The war to end all wars

### The end of pomp and glory

One British **front line** newspaper, the *Better Times*, spoke of the lack of excitement among exhausted and demoralized soldiers about the **armistice**. The paper's editor, Lieutenant-Colonel F J Roberts, commented that 'Most of us have been cured of any illusion we may have had about the pomp and glory of war, and know it for the vilest disaster that can befall mankind.'

In World War One, pomp and glory disappeared for good. Every soldier caught up in the slaughter had the misfortune to go to war at a time when the weapons of defence were vastly superior to the weapons of attack. But even during the war, new **tactics** and weapons evolved. By 1918, the fearsome **offensive** power of aeroplanes and tanks were being used. In a future war, this new **technology** would make the deadly **stalemate** of the trenches less likely.

## Good from bad

Not everything that came out of the war was bad. Nations had learned that, to wage war on such a grand scale, they had to harness the entire industrial strength of their nation. The need for men at the front and mass production of weaponry at home had led some nations to employ women in jobs previously held only by men. Women drove buses,

*Radio capabilities developed during World War One were soon put to use in civilian life. By the late 1920s, when this photo was taken, radio sets were common in American and western European homes.*

delivered coal, operated farm machinery and worked in **munitions** factories. Although they did not fight, they worked near to the front line as nurses, doctors and ambulance drivers. As a result, attitudes towards what women were capable of were changed forever.

Technological advances, accelerated greatly by the urgent needs of war, had peacetime benefits too. The science that built bombers was applied to passenger aircraft instead. Newly developed radio technology was used to create the world's first broadcasting organizations. Plastic surgery and blood **transfusions** became standard practices in **civilian** hospitals.

## Deadly lessons

By the time World War One was over, it was being referred to as the 'Great War' in recognition of the fact that human history had hitherto endured nothing like it. It was also called 'the war to end all wars' in the hope that its horrors would never be repeated.

But this was not to be. One of the greatest tragedies of World War One was that it led directly to another war that would be even more terrible in its slaughter. As early as 1920, a British journalist named Charles A'Court Repington had coined the term 'World War One'. Like many other perceptive people at the time, he knew that the struggle between the European nations was not yet over. Barely 20 years after the Great War ended, military technology had been honed to even greater levels of murderous efficiency. The weapons of World War Two would account for over four times as many casualties as 'the war to end all wars'.

*A dead German gunner lies beside his machine gun at the end of the war in 1918. Light machine guns were developed during the course of the conflict, making them more useful as offensive weapons. The weapons would be standard for **infantry** soldiers in World War Two, enhancing their killing power in direct combat.*

# Timeline

**1896**  First radio transmissions

**1898**  First portable X-ray machines used

**1900**  Discovery of four main blood groups completed

**1903**  First powered flight

**1904**  Field telephones first used (in Russo-Japanese War)

**1906**  Modern flame-thrower invented

**1914**  28 June: Assassination of Archduke Franz Ferdinand

28 July: Austria-Hungary declares war on Serbia

1 August: Germany declares war on Serbia's ally Russia

3 August: Germany declares war on France and invades Belgium

4 August: Britain declares war on Germany

14 August: French and German armies join battle in Northern France

26–30 August: Germans defeat Russians at Tannenberg

September: French army stops German advance at Battle of Marne

October/November: Trench systems established on Western Front

5 November: Allies declare war on the Ottoman Empire

**1915**  Italy joins Allies

Mark I tank developed in Britain

Renault F17 tank developed in France

Synchronized machine gun invented in Germany

3 January: First use of poisonous gas on Eastern Front (at Bolimov)

22 April : First use of poisonous gas on Western Front (at Ypres)

7 May: German U-boat sinks British liner *Lusitania*

31 May: First Zeppelin raid on London

30 July: First use (by Germany) of flame-thrower

**1916**  February–December: Battle of Verdun

31 May: Battle of Jutland

July–November: Battle of the Somme

15 September: First use (by British) of tanks

**1917**  Mustard gas introduced

6 April: US declares war on Germany

May: Allies adopt convoy system against German U-boat attacks

7 June: Explosives detonated in tunnels under German trenches at Messines, France

29 November: Tanks used successfully at Battle of Cambrai

17 December: Russia signs truce with Germany and withdraws from war

**1918**  Royal Air Force established in Britain

8 August: Allies launch final offensive against German army, which leads to German defeat

11 November: Armistice signed between Allies and Germany, ending World War One

# Further reading and places of interest

## Further reading
### *Books*

*History Through Poetry: World War One*, Paul Dowswell, Hodder Wayland, 2001
*Key Battles of World War I*, Fiona Reynoldson, Heinemann Library, 2001
*Oxford Illustrated History of the First World War*, Ed. Hew Strachan, OUP, 1998
*Weapons of the Trench War*, Anthony Saunders, Sutton Publishing, 1999
*The War in the Trenches*, Ole Steen Hansen, Hodder Wayland, 2000
*The World in Arms*, Time-Life History of the World, 1990
*The World War One Source Book*, Philip J. Haythornthwaite, Arms and Armour
    Press, 1996
*World War One*, Ed. Peter Furtado, Andromeda, 1993

### *Websites*

World War One website, recommended by the History Channel,
    with links to other sites:
    http://www.pitt.edu/~pugachev/greatwar/ww1.html
BBC World War One site:
    www.bbc.co.uk/history/wwone.shtml
Website of the Imperial War Museum, London, a major repository of
    World War One documents and artefacts:
    www.iwm.org.uk/
Website concerning involvements of United States soldiers in World War One:
    www.worldwar1.com/dbc/ghq1arm.htm

## Places of interest

Imperial War Museum, London

Royal Air Force Museum, Duxford

Bovington Tank Museum, Dorset

# Glossary

**ammunition** bullets, shells, missiles, grenades, and anything else fired during fighting

**armistice** agreement to stop fighting

**armor plating** thick metal sheets used as a protective covering, for example, on a tank or ship

**artillery** large guns that fire explosive shells

**barrage** barrier of heavy shell fire used to cover one's own side in an attack or to defend against an enemy attack

**barrel** tube of a gun through which ammunition is fired

**bayonet** metal blade attached to a gun

**blockade** use of warships to prevent other ships carrying goods or passengers from getting to and from enemy ports

**bunker** underground shelter

**canister** metal container that can hold gas or ammunition

**casualty** wounded or killed person

**caterpillar track** revolving steel band, made up of joined sections, that is used instead of wheels for vehicles that travel on rough ground or in mud

**cavalry** soldiers who fight on horseback

**civilian** person who is not in the armed forces

**colony** country or region ruled by another nation

**convoy** group of ships traveling together, often with an armed escort

**counterattack** response to an attack

**detonate** to make something explode

**dugout** covered area dug into a trench for shelter

**Eastern Front** important area of fighting in eastern Germany, Poland, and Galicia

**empire** territory, usually covering more than one country or area, that is ruled by an emperor or other ruler

**epidemic** disease spreading rapidly and affecting many people at once

**fortify** to make stronger or add defenses to something

**front line** foremost section of an army's defended territory, and thus the most exposed to the enemy

**fuse** device that sets off an explosion

**gangrene** condition where part of the body dies and then rots due to lack of blood circulation through the body tissues

**home front** situation of civilians in a nation at war

**howitzer** type of artillery that fires shells on a high trajectory

**incendiary bomb** bomb designed to set fire to buildings or other targets

**infantry** soldiers who fight on foot

**infestation** attack of disease or insects such as fleas or lice

**innovation** something new or changed

**latrine** toilet in a camp or trench

**magazine** container for bullets that is attached to a firearm

**maneuverable** easy to move, turn, or control in other ways

**minefield** area where explosive mines are laid

**munitions** ammunition, weapons, and other equipment for fighting wars

**musket** long-barreled firearm used mainly in the seventeenth and eighteenth centuries

**offensive** used for attacking; also means a large preplanned attack

**outflank** to advance around the side of an opposing army, to surround them or attack them from behind

**parapet** low wall built along the top of a trench to protect and hide troops

**periscope** instrument with which a person can see things from a concealed position, such as from a submerged submarine

**pneumonia** serious illness that inflames the lungs and fills them with liquid

**psychological** having to do with the mind

**reconnaissance** military effort to assess an enemy's strength and movement

**reinforcements** extra support, such as new men or weapons, brought into a battle

**retaliation** avenging one attack or injury with another

**rifle** long-barreled firearm with a rifled (spirally grooved) barrel that spins the bullet being fired, giving it longer range and greater accuracy

**round** ammunition for one shot

**semaphore** system of signaling using a flag in each hand, held in various positions to denote the letters of the alphabet

**shell** metal case containing explosives or other harmful materials

**shrapnel** form of explosive that violently scatters small pieces of metal; or, the pieces that are scattered

**sniper** gunman who fires from a hidden position

**stalemate** situation in which neither side in a conflict is able to defeat the other

**strategy** overall plan for dealing with a conflict or other situation

**strong point** defensive position on a battlefront that has extra fortifications or weapons

**tactic** use of troops and moves made in battle

**telegraph** device for sending messages along wires

**trajectory** path taken by an object as it flies through the air

**transfusion** injection of blood into a wounded person to replace blood lost in an injury

**turbine engine** engine driven by the flow of liquid, gas, or steam

**turret** small tower on a tank or ship that holds and protects guns and gunners

**velocity** speed of an object's movement

**war bond** certificate issued by a government during time of war to a citizen who lends money to the nation for the war effort. The bond promises repayment after the war with interest (extra money on top of the original amount of the loan).

**Western Front** area of fighting made up of two parallel lines of trenches—one German and one Allied—that stretched from the English Channel to the border of Switzerland

# Index

aeroplanes 32–33, 42, 43
    bombers 32, 43
    fighters 32, 33, 34, 35
    reconnaissance 20, 25, 32
Africa 6
airships 34–35
Allies 6, 9, 11, 15, 22, 29, 30
American Civil War 5, 7
artificial limbs 39
artillery 4, 5, 8, 9, 16, 18-21,
    32, 35, 39
Australia 33, 41
Austria-Hungary 6, 41

barbed wire 5, 8, 9, 10, 20,
    21, 26
barrages 20
Battle of Jutland 28, 29
Battle of the Somme 16, 18,
    26, 39
Battle of Waterloo 4
battlefronts 4, 5, 6, 7, 8, 9, 11,
    12, 16, 22, 24, 32, 35, 36,
    37, 38, 39, 41
battleships 5, 28, 29
bayonets 4, 13
Belgium 4, 8, 27
Bishop, William 33
blood transfusions 38–39, 43
bombs 32, 34, 35
Britain 6, 22, 25, 26, 28, 29, 30,
    31, 33, 34, 35, 41

Canada 33, 41
carrier pigeons 36, 37
casualties 4, 5, 7, 8, 9, 16, 18,
    22, 27, 28, 30, 33, 38, 39,
    40, 41, 43
cavalry 4, 5
Central Powers 6, 12
communications 8, 20, 36–37
convoys 31
Crimean War 5, 18

Ferdinand, Archduke 6
field mortars 14
field telephones 5, 10, 20,
    36, 37

flame-throwers 15
flying aces 33
forts 9
France 6, 8, 15, 20, 22, 25, 26,
    27, 29, 30, 33, 41

Gallipoli 8, 16
gas masks 21, 23
Germany 6, 8, 15, 25, 28, 29,
    30, 31, 40, 41
Gillies, Harold 39
grenades 15, 26

howitzers 5, 14, 18, 19

illness and infection 11, 12, 38, 40
Italy 27, 41

Kitchener, Lord 26

Little, Robert 33
Lusitania, the 30

machine guns 5, 8, 9, 16–17,
    26, 34, 43
    synchronized 32, 33
Mannock, Mick 33
Maxim, Hiram 17
medicine 38–39, 43
Middle East 6, 7
mines, land 29
mines, underground tunnel 15
mines, underwater 29
Morse code 36, 37
muskets 4, 5

New Zealand 39, 41

observation balloons 35
Ottoman Empire 6, 29, 41
Owen, Wilfred 23

Palestine 5
periscopes 10, 30
pistols 32
plastic surgery 39, 43
poisonous gas 14, 19, 20, 21,
    22–23, 38

radio 20, 36, 37, 42, 43
Repington, Charles A'Court 43
Richthofen, Baron von 33
Rickenbacker, Eddie 33
rifles 5, 12, 13, 25, 26
Roberts, Lt-Col F J 42
Royal Air Force 33
Russia 6, 25, 27, 29, 41
Russo-Japanese War 5, 7, 14, 36

secret codes 37
semaphore 21, 36
Serbia 6, 12
shell shock 39, 41
shells 8, 10, 12, 14, 16, 18, 19,
    20, 21, 22, 25, 26, 28, 38
shrapnel 12, 14, 18
submarines 29, 30–31
Swinton, Ernest 26

tanks 18, 26–27, 42
Tannenburg 16, 37
telegraph 36, 37
torpedoes 28, 29, 30, 31
transport 21, 24–25
    horse-drawn 24
    motorized, 24, 25
    rail 8, 24
trenches 7, 8–9, 10–11, 13, 14,
    15, 16, 17, 19, 20, 21, 27,
    33, 42

U-boats 30, 31
uniforms 4, 12
United States of America 6, 33, 41

Verdun 9, 19, 24, 27

war industry 18, 21, 34, 42, 43
warships 28–29, 30, 31
women workers 21, 42–43
World War Two 43
wounds 38, 39, 41

X-ray 38, 39

Zeppelin, Count von 34, 35
Zeppelins 34–35

# Titles in the *20th Century Perspectives* series include:

**20**th Century PERSPECTIVES

## The Rise of Modern China

Tony Allan

Hardback        0 431 11994 5

**20**th Century PERSPECTIVES

## The Changing Role of Women

Mandy Ross

Hardback        0 431 11997 X

**20**th Century PERSPECTIVES

## Weapons and Technology of World War I

Paul Dowswell

Hardback        0 431 11995 3

**20**th Century PERSPECTIVES

## Weapons and Technology of World War II

Windsor Chorlton

Hardback        0 431 11996 1

Find out about the other titles in this series on our website www.heinemann.co.uk/library